OFF TO JAMMU AND KASHMIR

SONIA MEHTA

PUFFIN BOOKS

An imprint of Penguin Random House

PUFFIN BOOKS

USA | Canada | UK | Ireland | Australia | New Zealand | India | South Africa | China | Singapore

Puffin Books is part of the Penguin Random House group of companies whose addresses can be found at global.penguinrandomhouse.com

Published by Penguin Random House India Pvt. Ltd
4th Floor, Capital Tower 1, MG Road,
Gurugram 122 002, Haryana, India

First published in Puffin Books by Penguin Random House India 2018

Text, design and illustrations copyright © Quadrum Solutions Pvt. Ltd 2018
Series copyright © Penguin Random House India 2018

Picture Credits

Title Page: A shikara on the Dal Lake (FotoGraphic/Shutterstock.com); P 7: The plains in Jammu and Kashmir (© Jochen Westermann from München, Germany (Wolken Berge Wasser Wiese) [CC BY-SA 2.0 (https://creativecommons.org/licenses/by-sa/2.0)], via Wikimedia Commons), Pine forests at foothills of the Himalayas (© Maxx786 [CC BY-SA 3.0 (https://creativecommons.org/licenses/by-sa/3.0)], via Wikimedia Commons), Pahalgam Valley (© KennyOMG (Own work) [CC BY-SA 3.0 (https://creativecommons.org/licenses/by-sa/3.0)], via Wikimedia Commons), Kashmir Valley (© Ishan Singal (Own work) [CC BY-SA 4.0 (https://creativecommons.org/licenses/by-sa/4.0)], via Wikimedia Commons), Himalayan range near Hemis National Park (© Akash Satpathy (Own work) [CC BY-SA 4.0 (https://creativecommons.org/licenses/by-sa/4.0)], via Wikimedia Commons), Karakoram Range (© Guilhem Vellut from Paris [CC BY-SA 2.0 (https://creativecommons.org/licenses/by-sa/2.0)], via Wikimedia Commons); P 9: Dal lake (Zephyr_p/Shutterstock.com); P 11: Kashmir stag (Hangul) (©Iasexam2018 (Own work) [CC BY-SA 4.0 (https://creativecommons.org/licenses/by-sa/4.0)], via Wikimedia Commons), Ibex (© 123shob123 (Own work) [CC BY-SA 4.0 (https://creativecommons.org/licenses/by-sa/4.0)], via Wikimedia Commons), Urial (© jonsson [CC BY 2.0 (http://creativecommons.org/licenses/by/2.0)], via Wikimedia Commons), Markhor (© Eric Kilby from Somerville, MA, USA [CC BY-SA 2.0 (https://creativecommons.org/licenses/by-sa/2.0)], via Wikimedia Commons); P 13: Kirimachi Temple Complex, Udhampur (© Malikbek (Own work) [CC BY 3.0 (http://creativecommons.org/licenses/by/3.0)], via Wikimedia Commons), Sonmarg (© Biswarup Bhattacharjee (Own work) [CC BY-SA 4.0 (https://creativecommons.org/licenses/by-sa/4.0)], via Wikimedia Commons); P 20: A group of snow bikers in Gulmarg (Chirawan Thaiprasansap/Shutterstock.com); P 30: Houseboats that are floating luxury hotels, Dal Lake (Tappasan Phurisamrit/Shutterstock.com), Vegetable vendors on Dal Lake (Darkydoors/Shutterstock.com); P 31: Inside a houseboat (FotoGraphic/Shutterstock.com), A living room inside a houseboat (FotoGraphic/Shutterstock.com); P 34: Young Buddhist monk rehearsing a dance performance at Hemis Monastery (FotoGraphic/Shutterstock.com); P 36: Vaishno Devi (© Raju Hardoi [CC BY-SA 3.0 (https://creativecommons.org/licenses/by-sa/3.0)], via Wikimedia Commons); P 38: Raghunath Temple (saiko3p/Shutterstock.com); P 39: Shankaracharya Temple (© Divya Gupta (Own work) [CC BY-SA 3.0 (https://creativecommons.org/licenses/by-sa/3.0)], via Wikimedia Commons), Hamdan Mosque (Tappasan Phurisamrit/Shutterstock.com); P 40: Farmers working in a field (CRS PHOTO/Shutterstock.com); P 49: Kashmiri men in pherans (Darkydoors/Shutterstock.com); P 49: Chitral Gol National Park (© Tahsin A Shah (Own work) [CC BY-SA 4.0 (https://creativecommons.org/licenses/by-sa/4.0)], via Wikimedia Commons)

The views and opinions expressed in this book are the author's own and the facts are as reported by her, which have been verified to the extent possible, and the publishers are not in any way liable for the same.

The information in this book is based on research from bona fide sites and published books and is true to the best of the author's knowledge at the time of going to print. The author is not responsible for any further changes or developments occurring post the publication of this book. This series is not a comprehensive representation of the states of India but is intended to give children a flavour of the lifestyles and cultures of different states. All illustrations are artistic representations only.

ISBN 9780143440918

Design and layout by Quadrum Solutions Pvt. Ltd
Printed at Repro India Limited

www.penguin.co.in

Hello Kids!

I'm so happy you are reading this book. India is an incredible country and there are lots of things about it that we never get to hear about.

I discovered India because my father was in the Indian army. He was posted to many places all over India—and we dutifully followed him. Can you imagine that by the time I was in the tenth standard, I had changed nine schools? Of course it was hard making new friends almost every year, but the good part was that I got to live in so many places. Right from Kerala, where I was born, to Kashmir, Jhansi, Shillong, Chandigarh, Goa . . . the list is long.

Every time I go to a new place, I feel amazed at how different each state is from the other—and yet, how similar. Did you know that we can see monuments from the Stone Age right here in India? Or that we have more than twenty official languages, and most Indians know three or four on an average? Or even that some of the world's most amazing scientific marvels were invented in India?

Oh, there are many, many, many fun and fantastic things about the states of India, which we simply must get to know.

So get your backpack ready, get set to meet some new friends and join me on a fun trip as we DISCOVER INDIA, STATE BY STATE.

I hope you enjoy reading this book as much as I have enjoyed writing it. I would love to hear from you. So do write to me at sonia.mehta@quadrumltd.com.

Lots of love,
Sonia Aunty

Mishki and Pushka have come to visit Earth from their home planet, Zoomba. They have never seen such an amazing place. Zoomba doesn't have trees and mountains and rivers like Earth does. But the people look exactly the same. When they come to Earth, they meet a sweet old man whom they call Daadu Dolma. Daadu Dolma shows them all the wonderful places in India and tells Mishki and Pushka all about them.

Mishki and Pushka can't believe what they see. They have seen a lot of Earth, but they have never, ever seen a place like India.

They are off to explore India state by state :)

Mishki

Mishki is a curious little girl. She is always asking loads of questions. On her home planet, she is always getting into trouble for poking her nose into things that are not her business.

Pushka

Pushka is Mishki's brother. He loves adventure. He is always ready to try a new challenge. Whether it's climbing a mountain, or diving into a cold, cold sea, he is up for it.

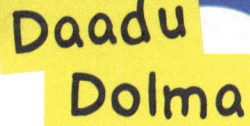
Daadu Dolma

Daadu Dolma is a wise old man who has lived on Earth longer than the mountains and seas. No one knows quite how old he is, but he certainly has been around. He knows everything about everything.

Mishki has been packing all day. Her bag is full of warm clothes, and she has made sure to take her camera.

'Daadu,' she says excitedly to Daadu Dolma, 'I have heard people calling Jammu and Kashmir "paradise on earth". What do they mean by that?'

'Well,' says Daadu, 'the beauty of Jammu and Kashmir is so breathtaking that people believe paradise must look like this. Both of you are in for a treat.'

'Well, what are we waiting for?' Pushka demands impatiently. He is in a hurry to go. They are all super excited because they are

OFF TO JAMMU AND KASHMIR!!!

A SNEAK PEEK

LAND AHOY!
About the land, water, rivers, mountains and seas.
page 6

LONG, LONG AGO

The story of the state.
page 14

TALK TIME
What language do the people speak?
page 20

A PEEP INTO THEIR LIFE
The music, dance and lifestyle of the people.
page 22

BRICKS AND STONES
Of houses, buildings and bridges.
page 28

STANDING STRONG
Famous monuments in Jammu and Kashmir.
page 32

WORKING HARD

What work do people do?
page 40

YUM YUM YUM
Food, food, food. What's the yummy food of Jammu and Kashmir?
page 44

WHAT TO WEAR?
The clothes they wear.
page 48

AUTOGRAPH, PLEASE?
Famous people—past and present.
page 50

ONCE UPON A TIME . . .
Stories from the state.
page 54

Land ahoy!

Yes! This state has beautiful lakes, mountains and valleys. That's what makes it so incredible. Come, let's start exploring.

I can already understand why this state is called paradise. What an amazing view!

NORTHERN CHARM

Jammu and Kashmir is in the northernmost region of India. It has two dramatic mountain ranges that give it its unique personality—the Karakoram range and the western part of the Himalayan range.

MANY NEIGHBOURS

For its neighbours, it has three foreign countries around its borders—China, Tibet and Pakistan. The Indian states of Himachal Pradesh and Punjab are its local neighbours.

ON THE MAP

To see exactly where **Jammu and Kashmir** is on the map of India, go to http://www.mapsofindia.com/maps/india/india-political-map.htm

SEVEN ZONES

The state could be said to have seven clear zones in terms of its land types.

- **The plain:** A dry area that has very few trees.
- **The foothills of the Himalayas:** This region has rocky areas that are millions of years old. The pine forests begin here.
- **The Pir Panjal range:** It was once a glacier but is now made of mountain peaks, deep valleys and meadows.
- **The Vale of Kashmir:** A deep basin, where most of the people in this state live.
- **The Great Himalayas zone:** It is made of dramatic peaks and sharp valleys.
- **The upper Indus River valley:** It has deep gorges and mountain masses, including the famous Nanga Parbat. The sunlight here is so sharp that it's quite hard to bear.
- **The Karakoram range:** It has some of the world's highest peaks, such as K2.

LOVELY LADAKH

Ladakh is a region in the Karakoram range that has one of the most spectacular landscapes in the world. Leh and Kargil are its two main districts, and they are so high up in the mountains that you have to acclimatize yourself when you're there. It isn't easy to breathe because the air is so thin. But the people who live there are sturdy and strong.

RIVER RUSH

Some of India's most important rivers water this state as they rush down the mountains. The Indus River is born in Tibet and comes flowing down from the Himalayas. The Chenab, the Jhelum, the Doda, the Dras, the Markha and the Tawi are the other main rivers that meander through the state, watering fields and valleys along the way.

BRRRRRRRRR!

As you can imagine, it gets very, very cold in this state—especially in the higher reaches. During winters, many parts get completely snowbound. But summertime sees valleys bursting with delightful flowers, and the weather is wonderful.

THE LAKES OF KASHMIR

Kashmir has some really lovely lakes that are famous all over the world. The most popular is Dal Lake. Dotted with lotus flowers and houseboats that tourists love, Dal Lake is Kashmir's pride. Some of the other lakes are Wular and Manasbal. A few of these also offer water sports.

HIDDEN RIVERS

Can you find the state's rivers hidden in this grid?

T	A	W	I	H	G	F	D	S	A
A	D	C	H	E	N	A	B	O	T
S	F	G	H	J	K	L	P	I	R
A	J	H	E	L	U	M	Y	U	E
S	D	F	I	N	D	U	S	Q	W
F	D	O	D	A	G	H	J	K	L
D	M	N	B	V	D	R	A	S	Z
S	Q	M	A	R	K	H	A	X	C

FOREST FABLES

This state has some incredible forests. Its woodlands are full of lovely trees, like deodars, cedars, blue pines, walnut trees, willows, elms, firs, poplars, pines and spruces. Many of them change colour with the seasons. What a lovely sight that must be.

Pine forest in Sonmarg

Kashmiri saffron is very famous. In fact, almost all the saffron grown in India comes from Kashmir.

CROP HOP

Even though there are so many mountains, farmers still manage to grow quite a lot of crops. They slice the mountainsides into terraces and grow rice, corn, millet, wheat, barley, pulses and mustard in different seasons. There are also some lovely orchards where fruits like apples, peaches and cherries are grown!

FUN FACTS

State animal
Kashmir stag (hangul)

State flower
Lotus

State bird
Black-necked crane

State tree
Chinar

WILD AND WONDERFUL

Markhor

With so much forestland comes lots of wildlife. The rare snow leopard, the Siberian ibex, the Ladakh urial, the rare Kashmir stag (also called the hangul), the endangered markhor, black and brown bears and many species of birds roam these forests.

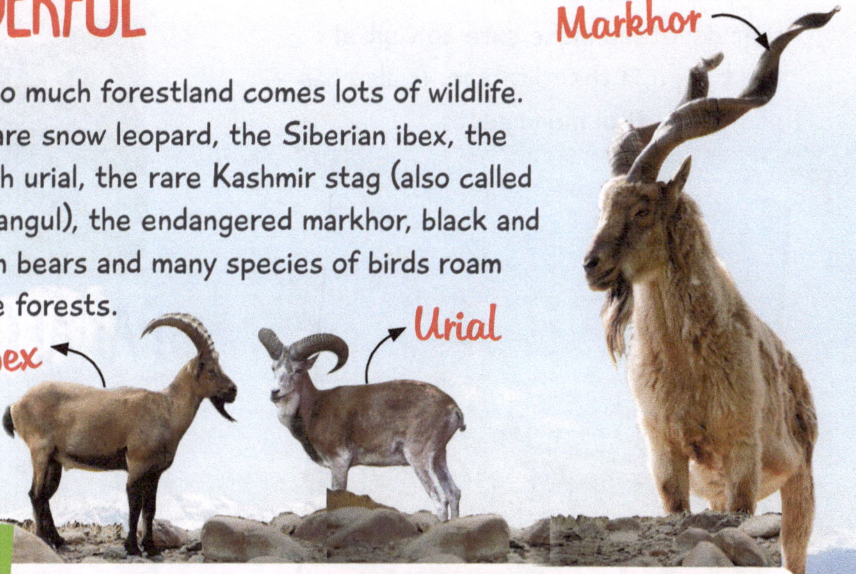

Snow leopard

Ibex

Urial

WHAT'S ODD?

Each row below has one word that doesn't belong. Can you help Mishki find them?

| Cherry | Apple | Orange | Potato | Peach |

| Walnut | Coconut | Willow | Elm | Fir |

| Bear | Turtle | Urial | Stag | Ibex |

??? ?

CITY CITY BANG BANG

Boats known as shikaras on Dal Lake

SRINAGAR

This lovely city is the state capital. It sits prettily on the banks of the Jhelum. The beautiful Dal Lake is also here. Srinagar is hugely popular with tourists.

JAMMU

The city of Jammu is called the city of temples by some. It has many temples that devotees make sure to visit at least once in their lifetime. It also has some beautiful monuments.

Mabarak Mandi Palace

PAHALGAM

Known best for its stunning natural beauty, Pahalgam is very popular with tourists. It has lots of hotels and many places where visitors go for horse riding, trekking, golf and other fun activities.

UDHAMPUR

This city has been named after a king called Raja Udham Singh. It has a rich history. An underground river called the Devika (believed to be the Ganga's sister) flows here.

SONMARG

Here's another city that nature has blessed. People come here when they want to go trekking in the mountains. Pilgrims also halt here on their way to religious places higher up in the Himalayas.

Skiing in Gulmarg

GULMARG

Known as a skiers' paradise, you can get some great snowy action during winter in Gulmarg. People also call it 'the meadow of flowers' because of the beautiful flowers that bloom here in summer.

LEH

Leh is like a jewel in the Ladakh region of the state. It's an adventure just getting to Leh. Monasteries, mountains, palaces and breathtaking views are what you'll get to see here.

Long, long ago

Well, Jammu and Kashmir has a very complex history. There have been many kings from different regions who have ruled. But that's what it makes it interesting.

Wow! I have never seen so much natural beauty in just one place. Daadu, what is the state's history like?

AS OLD AS OLD CAN BE

According to legend, the area where Kashmir is today was once a vast lake. A monk named Kashyapa reclaimed the land from the lake. The land was called Kashyapamar—later coming to be known as Kashmir.

Some people believe that Jammu was established by Raja Jambu Lochan in the fourteenth century. It is said that one day, while hunting on the banks of the Tawi River, he saw a goat and a lion drinking water next to each other. He was so stunned by this sight that he took it to be a sign. He established a town in his name. And so, Jambu came into being. Later, this turned into Jammu.

IN THE TIME OF THE MAHABHARATA

People believe that Kashmir was once ruled by the Gonand dynasty. King Gonand fought a battle against Lord Krishna, during which he and his son Damodar were killed. But Krishna, instead of taking over the kingdom, made Damodar's wife, Yashowati, the queen. Soon she gave birth to a prince. After that, more than thirty Gonand kings are believed to have ruled Kashmir.

A PANDAVA CONNECTION

There is no clear evidence, but people believe that after the Gonand dynasty, the descendants of the Pandavas ruled this region too! In those days, this region included parts of Afghanistan as well. Imagine that!

HIDDEN WORDS

RAJA JAMBU LOCHAN is such a long name. Can you make smaller words by mixing up the letters of the name? Pushka has made one.

JAR
_____
_____
_____
_____
_____
_____
_____

KUSHANA TIMES

At some point, a Kushana king called Kanishka ruled over Kashmir. He was a Buddhist, and under his rule, Buddhism spread to Turkey and Afghanistan.

HUNS ATTACK

The Huns had entered India through the passes in the Himalayas. Unable to go too deep into India, they turned towards Kashmir. A fierce king called Mehrkul attacked Kashmir. He was known to be ruthless. In those days, Kashmir was mainly occupied by Kashmiri Pandits, who were devotees of Lord Shiva. Influenced by the Pandits, Mehrkul became calmer and even began to follow Shiva.

A QUEEN TO REMEMBER

For many years, Kashmir was ruled by a queen named Queen Didda. Having lost her husband, King Khemgupta, she acted

Gold coins with Didda's seal

as ruler in place of her son, who was too young. She ruled for many years and was widely respected. Some years into her rule, Muhammad of Ghazni, a fierce ruler from Afghanistan, attacked. She and her army successfully fended him off.

MANY INVADERS

Over the next hundreds of years, many invaders entered and plundered Kashmir. The region was torn with unrest and war. However, these warlords, like Sikander, Saifuddin, Fateh Shah, Moosa Raina and Mir Hajjar Khan, also brought with them their own culture, religion and architecture.

RHYME TIME

Mishki is writing a poem about Kashmir's famous kings and queens. She needs five words that rhyme with the three words given below.

R U L E _____ _____ _____ _____ _____

A T T A C K _____ _____ _____ _____ _____

Q U E E N _____ _____ _____ _____ _____

SIKHS ON THE SCENE

The Sikh ruler, Maharaja Ranjit Singh, attacked Kashmir and defeated the Pathans. For many subsequent years, Kashmir was a part of Ranjit Singh's empire.

MONGOL MIGHT

A fierce Mongol warrior called Dulucha entered Kashmir through the mountain passes. His attack was savage, and he is said to have massacred anyone who came in his way. He destroyed palaces, monuments and temples. He was followed by Pathani warlords, who ruled with an iron fist.

THE INDEPENDENCE FIGHT

All through this time, Indians were rebelling against the British. They wanted their independence. There were continuous protests across the country. Finally, in 1947, the British went back home, and India was independent at last.

THE BRITISH IMPACT

By this time, the British had occupied almost all of India. They had made it a British colony. They easily defeated Ranjit Singh's Sikh army, and took over Kashmir as well. But the British were not too interested in managing this region. They sold Kashmir to Maharaja Gulab Singh of the Doghra dynasty for just seventy-five lakhs of rupees. The Doghra dynasty ruled for many years.

KASHMIR CHOOSES

India was divided into two countries—India and Pakistan. Maharaja Hari Singh, who was the ruler of Kashmir during that period, decided that he would attach his state to India. So Jammu and Kashmir officially became a state of India.

Talk time

Jammu and Kashmir is absolutely delightful, Daadu. Come, let's meet some people and talk to them.

We can do that right away. The people of Kashmir are very friendly. But we will have to learn a little about their language. Let's find out more.

MANY LANGUAGES

There have been so many rulers in this state over the centuries that there are now many languages and dialects that people speak. In different parts of the state, people speak different languages. Urdu, Dogri, Kashmiri, Hindi, Punjabi, Ladakhi, Balti, Gojri, Pashto and Shina are just some.

LET'S LEARN SOME KASHMIRI PHRASES:

- How are you? = Tohy ch'ivaa vaarai?
- Fine, thank you! And you? = Vaarai, shukriyaa!
  Tiu tohy?
- Long time, no see! = Variya kaal gov na myelnasi!
- What's your name? = Twahi kyaa ch'u naav?
- My name is Mishki = Me ch'u naav Mishki
- Where are you from? = Tohy katik ch'v?
- Pleased to meet you = Me sapiuz k'oshee
  twahu meelit'
- Sorry = Maap' keuriv
- Please = Meharbenee
- Thank you = Shukriyaa

MATCH THEM RIGHT

Pushka is practising Kashmiri.
Help him match the English phrases
to their Kashmiri translations.

How are you?	Maap' keuriv
Sorry	Meharbenee
What's your name?	Shukriyaa
Please	Tohy ch'ivaa vaarai?
Thank you	Twahi kyaa ch'u naav?

A peep into their life

Well, some things in the culture are similar to those in neighbouring states, but some things are unique to Jammu and Kashmir. Come, let's find out some more.

This is a really interesting state, Daadu. Is it very different from the states around it?

A WONDERFUL MIX

This state has had a very colourful history. This is why its culture is very diverse and colourful too! The people living here are a wonderful mix of Sikhs, Buddhists, Hindus and Muslims. You'll find that the music, dance and celebrations reflect this diversity.

LET THE MUSIC PLAY

Music is everywhere in Jammu and Kashmir. The musical instruments from here are unique too! The rebab, santoor, nagara, sitar and *tumbakhnar* are some of the most popular.

Santoor

Tumbakhnar

Sitar

Nagara

Rebab

LADISHAH

In this style of music, singers travel from village to village, singing songs about life. Sung mainly during the harvest season, this music addresses issues related to villages—political or social.

CHAKRI

This form of folk music is hugely popular among the local people in the valleys. Through songs, performers tell stories of unrequited love and fairy tales. The songs often end with a dance called *rouf*. Women sing it during bridal henna ceremonies too!

SUFIANA

Sufi music is a mix of prayer and meditation. Performers seem to go into a trance while singing. This music originated in Persia, but over centuries, artists and performers have added their own special touches to it.

CHANCE TO DANCE

HAFIZA

This traditional dance is usually performed during weddings, to an accompaniment of Sufi music.

BHAND PATHER

Also called Bhand Jashna (festival of clowns), this is Kashmir's traditional folk theatre, enacted during festivals and other celebrations. It is a mix of drama and dance, and the subject is often a depiction of social traditions—both good and bad.

ROUF

This traditional dance is performed during weddings. Women dance in groups wearing traditional finery.

KUD

Performers dance to give thanks to the gods for a good harvest and a happy life. Usually taking place at night, the dancers perform complex, intricate moves. Young and old join in, and everyone has a wonderful time.

ALL MIXED UP

Pushka and Mishki want to remember the names of the dances. But they are mixed up! Can you unjumble the words for them?

AAFZIH – _____

FOUR – _____

DUK – _____

HEMIS

Along with being the name of a place in Leh, this is a Buddhist festival that celebrates the birthday of Buddhist guru Padmasambhava. Held in the courtyard of a large monastery in Ladakh, the monks recall the time their guru fought evil demons. Lamas wear masks and perform a dance that depicts the victory of good over evil. It's great fun to watch!

URS

Urs in Hamdan Mosque

Urs is a festival celebrated in many states, but it's particularly big in Jammu and Kashmir. Also called Ziarat, this festival is held to honour Muslim saints. Often held at the shrines of these great saints, people of all faiths come to pray during this time.

VAISHNO DEVI

This is a three-month-long festival during which devotees pray to Goddess Vaishno Mata at the famous Vaishno Devi temple.

EID-UL-FITR

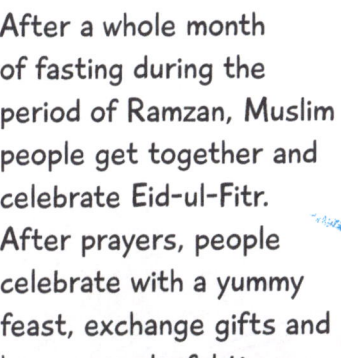

After a whole month of fasting during the period of Ramzan, Muslim people get together and celebrate Eid-ul-Fitr. After prayers, people celebrate with a yummy feast, exchange gifts and have a wonderful time.

DUSSEHRA

The festival of Dussehra, which is a big celebration in many parts of India, is extra special in Jammu. Giant effigies of Ravana, Meghanada and Kumbhakarana (three characters from the Ramayana who are considered to be evil) are stuffed with crackers. Fiery arrows are shot into the air and the effigies light up. People celebrate the victory of good over evil during this dramatic festival.

FESTIVAL MATCH

Can you match the name of the festival to its description?

The end of a month of fasting   Hemis

A three-month festival   Dussehra

The victory of good over evil   Vaishno Devi

A festival also called Ziarat   Eid-ul-Fitr

A big Buddhist festival   Urs

Bricks and stones

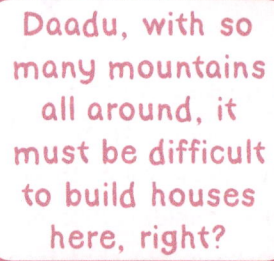

Daadu, with so many mountains all around, it must be difficult to build houses here, right?

You're right about that. But people have figured out what kind of houses are best, in keeping with the climate and local materials too. And there are some really interesting ones. Let's take a look.

BATTLING THE COLD

The main thing for people living here has always been to try and keep homes warm during the freezing winters. So people build their homes using thick brick and stone, with mud plaster covering it all. These are actually light materials, so in case of an earthquake, no one will get hurt.

MELTING SNOW

People also have to make sure that the melting snow on their rooftop doesn't leak into the house. This is why roofs are slanting, so the snow rolls right off the roof. They're made out of timber, which prevents water leakage.

Slanting roofs

Kaieni

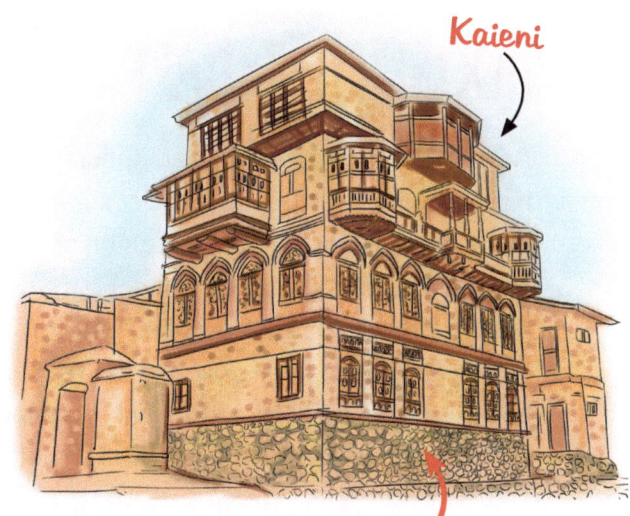

MANY FLOORS

Another interesting thing is that because the region is mountainous, there isn't much flat land for houses to be built horizontally. So people built tall houses that had steep staircases. Often they would have a room right on top, called a *kaieni*, that was as an attic or a playroom for children.

KEEPING WARM

Most homes have a traditional heater called a *bukhari*. Placed right in the centre of the main room, the bukhari is heated with coal or firewood, and it keeps everyone nice and warm. Sounds toasty, doesn't it?

A bukhari

HOUSEBOAT HAPPINESS

Among the most amazing and special things about Kashmir are its houseboats. Because it has so many lakes, many people live on or on the edge of these lakes. They build houseboats, which are proper houses that have rooms and furniture all inside a boat. Even now, there are many houseboats on the lakes of Kashmir. Many are houseboat hotels, meant for tourists.

People say that the first boats were built as homes for British people because the maharaja of Jammu and Kashmir at that time didn't allow foreigners to buy land. So they made their homes on the water.

What an amazing life! I would love to live on a houseboat and go to school in a shikara.

LIFE ON THE LAKE

Many houseboat dwellers are fishermen, who make their living by fishing these waters. Some even grow vegetables on the lake. They grow these on a mat that is woven from weeds. It is kept on the water, and vegetables like cabbages, spinach and pumpkins actually grow on it.

HOME ON THE WATER

A bathroom inside a houseboat

Houseboats have all the rooms a house does: a drawing room, bedrooms, a kitchen and bathrooms. Most houseboats have balconies or verandas with steps that lead down to the water. Houseboat owners also have smaller boats called shikaras. People use shikaras to go to the mainland for anything they need.

A living room in a houseboat

Families have lived in houseboats for generations. Now, many rent them out to tourists and have made some houseboats super luxurious.

SHIKARA SURPRISE

Look at these two pictures. They seem to be identical. Or are they? Pushka is surprised to find that there are ten differences between the two. Can you find them all?

31

Standing strong

I am convinced that Jammu and Kashmir must have some really amazing monuments.

Oh, yes! We are going to see some incredible monuments—palaces, forts, temples, mosques and monasteries. You'll find the architecture here very different from that in the rest of India.

PALACE PERFECT

LEH PALACE

In the heart of breathtaking Leh is the Leh Palace. It was built in the classic Tibetan architectural style by the ruler of this region at that time, King Sengge Namgyal. With nine floors, the palace housed the royal family on the top floors, while stables, storage rooms and the servants' quarters were all on lower floors. There were no lifts in those days, so imagine how tough it must have been to constantly climb all those stairs!

PARI MAHAL

Pari Mahal means 'fairy palace'—and it certainly is one. It was built by a Mughal prince named Dara Shikoh. The palace once housed a great library. It was then converted into a place for the study of astronomy. It is perched on a mountaintop from where you can see Dal Lake.

BAG-E-BAHU FORT

This is probably one of the oldest palace forts in Jammu and Kashmir. It was built by a king called Raja Bahulochan over 3000 years ago. The kings from the Doghra dynasty added on to it. Sitting on the banks of the Tawi River, this palace fort has lovely terraces, gardens and waterfalls.

LOST IN THE MAZE

Mishki and Pushka have lost their way while exploring the palace gardens. Can you help them find their way out?

MAGNIFICENT MONASTERIES

Jammu and Kashmir has some of the north's most stunning monasteries. Because of its Tibetan influence, many Buddhist monks still live in these monasteries.

THIKSEY MONASTERY

Thiksey Gompa (Buddhist monasteries are called *gompas*) is one of the oldest monasteries in the region. It was founded by a monk, Spon Paldan Sherab, hundreds of years ago. Even now, many monks live, pray and meditate here.

HEMIS MONASTERY

This is said to be the largest monastery in Ladakh. It has more than 200 wings, and it is said that more than a thousand monks live in each wing. Do the math and you will be amazed at how many monks must live here! Getting there is an adventure in itself. But once you are there, you will get to see beautiful Buddhist art and architecture.

Alchi Monastery

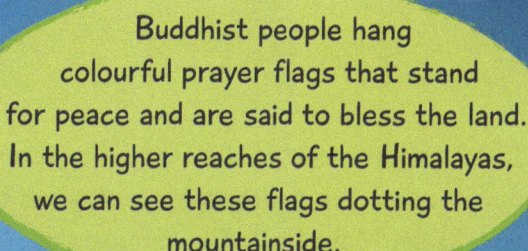

Buddhist people hang colourful prayer flags that stand for peace and are said to bless the land. In the higher reaches of the Himalayas, we can see these flags dotting the mountainside.

ALCHI MONASTERY

On the banks of the Indus River is this monastery, also known as Alchi Choskor. It was built by a famous translator of Buddhist texts, Rinchen Zangpo. Very ancient and with several temples inside it, this monastery is one of the very few that sits on flat ground.

WHAT COMES NEXT?

The prayer flags below follow a certain pattern. Can you say which colour each of the uncoloured flags should be?

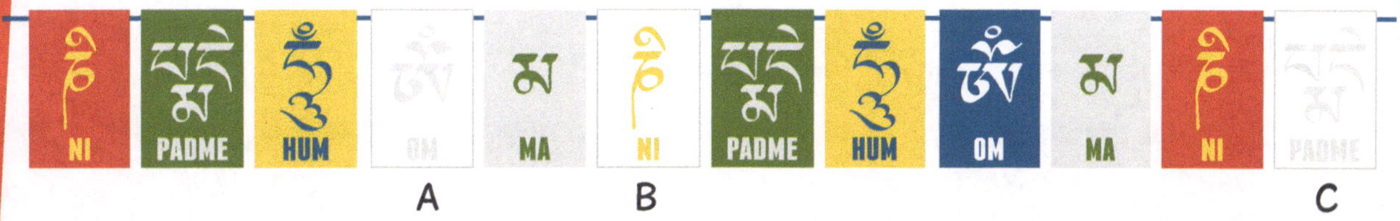

NI | PADME | HUM | OM | MA | NI | PADME | HUM | OM | MA | NI | PADME

A   B   C

TIME TO PRAY

VAISHNO DEVI TEMPLE

This temple is one of the most important for devotees of the goddess Mata Vaishno Devi, also called Mata Rani. The temple sits high on a hilltop, and devotees have to trudge up thousands of steps over a distance of nearly 14 kilometres to get there. It is said that more than eight million people visit this temple every year.

Inside Mata Vaishno Devi shrine

AMARNATH TEMPLE

The ice Shiv ling inside the cave

This is a cave temple that is devoted to Lord Shiva. It has a massive Shiv ling (the symbol of Lord Shiva) made of ice. Legend goes that Lord Shiva held the secret of immortality. His wife Parvati begged him to tell her the secret. Lord Shiva finally agreed—but decided he would do it in a quiet, secret place. He chose a cave. And this is the cave in which the Amarnath Temple is today.

AALI MASJID

This is a really ancient mosque built during the rule of Sultan Hassan Shah, as far back as the 1400s. Over the centuries, different dynasties, including the Mughals and the Doghras, added to and restored this mosque, which is a lovely example of Kashmiri architecture.

JAMIA MASJID

Sultan Sikandar is believed to have built this amazing mosque over a thousand years ago. It is a beautiful building that can fit more than 30,000 people at one time. There are soaring towers (called minars) and pillars that make this a beautiful structure. People come from all over India to pray here.

RAGHUNATH TEMPLE

This temple is devoted to Lord Rama. It is a magnificent structure with walls that are covered with sheets of gold. A maharaja of Jammu and Kashmir, Raja Gulab Singh, ordered its construction over a hundred years ago. There are lakhs of *shaligrams* (holy stones) embedded in the walls. There is even a library of rare Sanskrit scriptures. This temple is a must see!

HAZRATBAL MOSQUE

Sitting on the edge of Dal Lake, this lovely mosque is made of glowing white marble that reflects magically in the waters of the lake. Of great importance is a preserved strand of hair, which devotees believe is the hair of Prophet Muhammad himself. On special occasions, the hair is brought out and displayed, while thousands come to pray at this mosque.

SHANKARACHARYA TEMPLE

This is a really ancient temple that pays homage to Shankaracharya, who people believe was a seeker of truth. He came to Kashmir and tried to revive the ancient religion of Sanatan Dharma, which is what Lord Rama and Lord Krishna are said to have practised.

HAMDAN MOSQUE

This is said to be one of the most important places for prayer in Kashmir. Something amazing about this mosque is that people believe that the builders didn't use a single nail or even a screw while constructing it, even though it is made entirely of wood. Wow! There are ornate chandeliers and wall pieces that make this a very beautiful place to pray in.

PRAYING HARD

Mishki and Pushka are praying hard. Can you find their exact shadow?

A

B

C

D

E

F

Working hard

I have decided to live in Jammu and Kashmir for the rest of my life.

Oh, yeah? What will you do for a living then?

Well, Pushka, why not find out what occupations people have here? That way you can decide what you'll be really good at!

FARMER, FARMER, WHAT DO YOU GROW?

Farmers here have very busy lives indeed. They grow different things at different times of the year. So there are summer crops, like rice, millet, pulses and cotton, and there are spring crops, like wheat and barley. They have to carve out fields on the slopes and make terraced farms—very hard work, all right!

THE FRUIT OF THEIR LABOUR

There are many orchards in Jammu and Kashmir because the soil and climate are perfect to grow fruits like apples, peaches, pears and cherries. A lot of people work in these orchards. Many also work in factories where the fruits are turned into jams or sauces.

SAFFRON SONG

As we saw earlier, Kashmir is famous for the saffron grown here. There are many, many farmers who cultivate saffron. It's the occupation of thousands of people, but it's hard work because you have to be very careful to produce this spice just right.

CROSSWORD FUN

Help Mishki and Pushka solve this crossword!

ACROSS

1. Something that Kashmir is really famous for.

6. Something yummy that is made of fruit and is spread on bread.

7. A five-letter fruit that begins with 'P'.

8. The place where many fruits grow.

DOWN

2. This crop is grown during summer in Kashmir.

3. These people work hard on fields to grow crops.

4. It's made from different fruits, often tomatoes, and adds flavour to food.

7. A fruit that rhymes with 'dare'.

CREATIVE CRAFTSPEOPLE

The people of Jammu and Kashmir are very good with their hands! They weave, carve and paint the most amazing things, which are famous all over the world.

Silk factory employees

SUPER SERICULTURE

Sericulture—the breeding of silkworms for producing silk—is a big business here too! There are many silkworm farms, where a lot of people work to create silk, which is turned into beautiful, soft fabric.

TOURIST TRENDS

As you can imagine, tourism is a really huge business here and is probably the most important of all occupations. This is because people from all over the world visit this state to enjoy its spectacular beauty. This is why there are a lot of people working in hotels and restaurants, as well as airline and travel agencies!

CARVERS OF WOOD

Wood carving is a big industry here. There is a lot of lovely wood, like teak and timber, available in plenty. For generations, families have been in the business of creating delightful objects like lamps, frames and furniture.

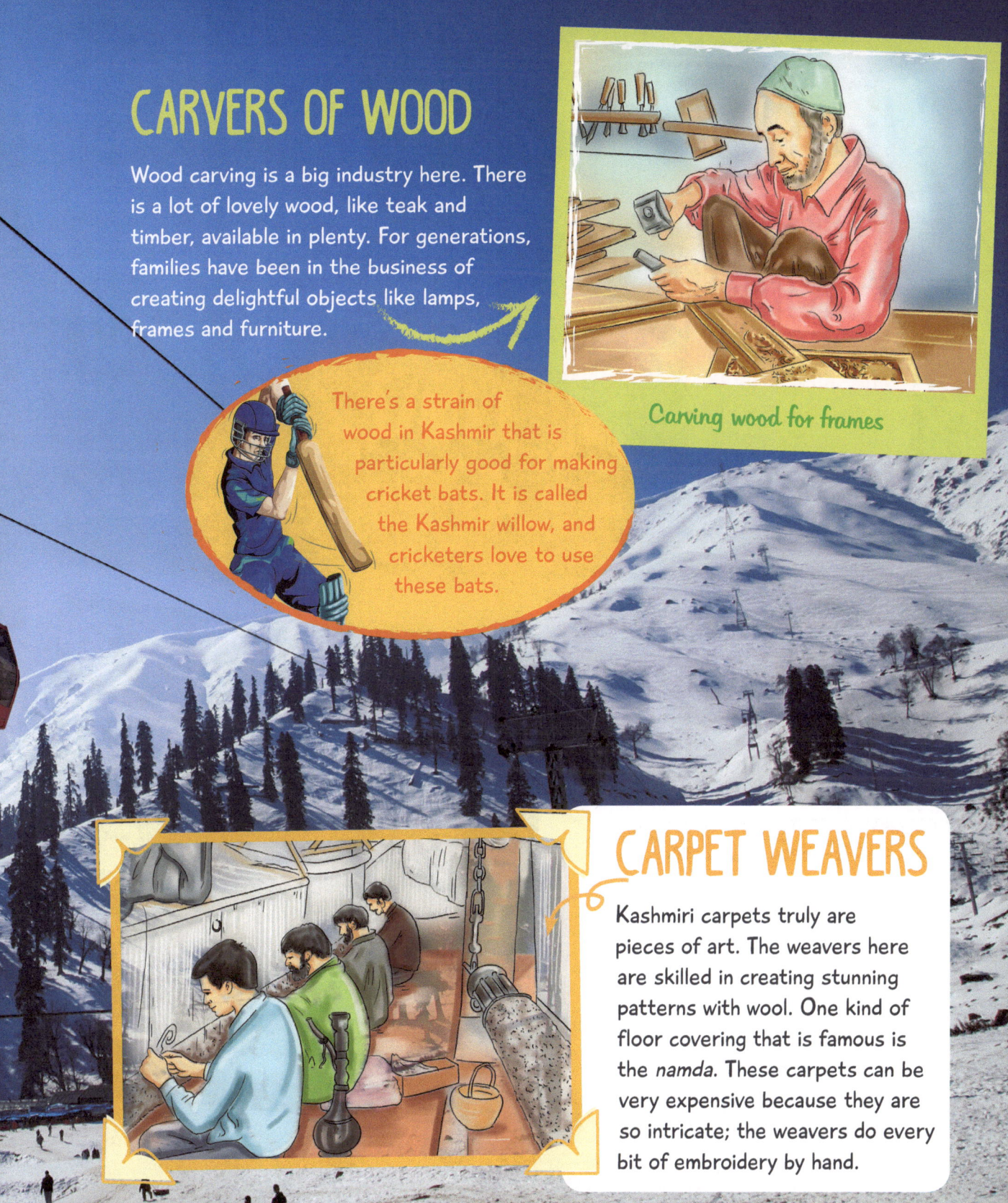

Carving wood for frames

There's a strain of wood in Kashmir that is particularly good for making cricket bats. It is called the Kashmir willow, and cricketers love to use these bats.

CARPET WEAVERS

Kashmiri carpets truly are pieces of art. The weavers here are skilled in creating stunning patterns with wool. One kind of floor covering that is famous is the *namda*. These carpets can be very expensive because they are so intricate; the weavers do every bit of embroidery by hand.

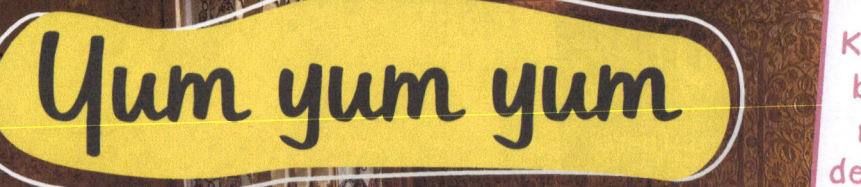

Yum yum yum

That is the fragrance of Kashmiri spices. You get the best spices here, and they make the food absolutely delicious. Want to try some? Come along!

Daadu, what is that scrumptious smell? It's making my mouth water.

WAZWAN— A ROYAL FEAST

This is a grand traditional meal that consists of as many as thirty-six courses. The head chef, called the *vasta waza*, presides over the preparation. Guests are made to sit in groups of four. The meal begins with everyone washing their hands in a basin that is given to everyone. The art of cooking this meal is passed down from generation to generation. No wedding is complete without this meal.

Tash-t-nari, the ceremonial vessel that is used to wash one's hands

Thirty-six-course wazwan treat

BAKARKHANI

No typical Kashmiri meal can be complete without this delicious bread. This is a crisp, round bread that is baked in layers and sprinkled with crunchy sesame seeds.

SHEERMAL

This is a sweet naan-like bread that is baked in a home-style oven called a tandoor. Almost all homes here have this contraption. Do you know what makes sheermal tasty? Instead of using water while making the dough, people use thick, wholesome milk. No wonder it tastes so rich.

LYODUR TSCHAMAN

Vegetarians, it's your turn! Made from cottage cheese and with a thick gravy, this is one of Kashmir's most popular vegetarian dishes.

MODUR PULAO

This utterly delectable rice dish is sweet and very fragrant. It's also very rich, filled with cinnamon, milk, ghee, sugar, cashew nuts, almonds and green cardamom. It certainly sounds divine!

NADUR CHURMA

We know that the lotus flower grows in plenty in this state. The stems of the flower make for some yummy dishes. Lotus stems are fried till they are crisp and crunchy and taste as good as (or better than) French fries. This dish is also called nadur monj.

LYDE

Time for dessert! Lydes are sweet wheat balls that have sugar in them and are fried. Kashmiris love to have these with tea.

SHUFTA

People love having this dessert during the winter months because it is known to generate heat and keep people warm. Like a lot of other Kashmiri food, this one too has plenty of dry fruits and, of course, saffron.

YAKHNI

This is a yummy meat dish that is very popular. It has a delectable gravy made of curd and spices, and flavoured with saffron. Weddings and celebrations aren't complete without this.

Yakhni's famous cousin is the yakhni pulao. Just as tasty.

KAHWAH TEA

This is a famous tea that people serve during special occasions. People say its origins lie in an ancient Arab drink. It is a special kind of brew that has green tea, spices, saffron and walnuts or almonds. Delicious!

A samovar, which is a tea pot

NOON CHAI/SHEER CHAI

The people of Jammu and Kashmir love their tea. And why not? They have some unbelievable flavours. Noon tea is a slightly salted tea. It is made of green tea, milk, salt and a pinch of soda powder. Imagine that! Ever had salty tea?

FOOD CODE

Can you crack Pushka's code?
He is trying to tell Daadu something.

| 1 = L | 2 = T | 3 = E |
| 5 = U | 7 = S | 8 = A |

1 3 2   5 7   3 8 2

__ __ __   __ __   __ __ __

What to wear?

Oh, yes! They have to. You've seen how cold it can get here. Everyone has clothes made of wool, which they can wear on top of their regular clothes.

I'm all set to dress up in some of the lovely clothes I've been seeing. People seem to dress very warm here.

PRETTY IN PHERANS

Pheran

The *pheran* is the most common clothing that women wear. It is a loose, flowing garment, usually made of wool. It has some lovely embroidery around the neck, and that's what makes it so special. It even has pockets, which makes things very convenient!

COVERING THEIR HEADS

Most traditional Hindu women cover their heads with a scarf called the *taranga*. Muslim women wear a slightly different headgear, the *kasaba* or abaya. Unmarried girls wear tight caps on their heads, which are heavily embroidered. Everything looks so pretty.

Embroidered caps

Taranga

LOTS OF JEWELLERY

You'll see women in Jammu and Kashmir dressed up for special occasions. They wear the most stunning silver jewellery like necklaces, bracelets and anklets.

PHERANS FOR MEN TOO!

Men wearing pherans

Men also wear pherans, just like women do. These are not as heavily decorated but are like coarse throws over their regular clothes. Muslim men wear loose kurtas with salwars, often called Pathan suits because that's what their ancestors must have worn in Persia.

HANDY HEADGEAR

Headgear is important. Depending on where they are from, men wear either a turban or a cap. Apart from being a cultural habit, it helps with the cold too!

A fur cap

PASHMINA SHAWLS

These are super fine shawls that are unique to this state. The wool comes from a special type of mountain goat. People say that when woven, the material is so fine that it can pass through a ring. Both men and women use these shawls, either to wrap around themselves or as a cummerbund, which is a sort of thick sash wrapped around the waist.

Pashmina goats

Autograph, please?

Daadu, tell us about the famous people from this state, please. There must be quite a few.

Yes, there are! This state has produced some super talented people. Many have moved away to other states or countries. Let's meet some of them.

USTAD ALLARAKHA QURESHI

Known simply as Ustad Allarakha, this tabla maestro was a world-famous musician, known as perhaps the greatest tabla player of all time. He has won many international and Indian honours. His son, Ustad Zakir Hussain, is also an incredibly talented tabla player.

LALLESHWARI

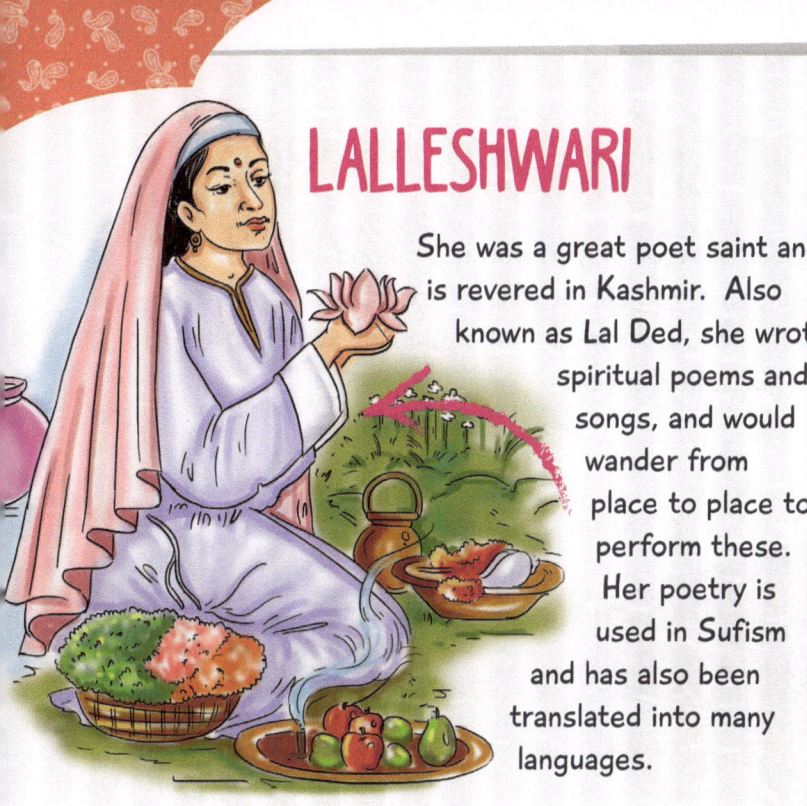

She was a great poet saint and is revered in Kashmir. Also known as Lal Ded, she wrote spiritual poems and songs, and would wander from place to place to perform these. Her poetry is used in Sufism and has also been translated into many languages.

HABBA KHATOON

Known by some as the Nightingale of Kashmir, Habba Khatoon lived many centuries ago. She was a beautiful woman, married to the ruler of Kashmir. When her husband was captured by enemies, she renounced everything and became an ascetic. She wrote many songs and poems that became very famous.

KUNDAN LAL SAIGAL

Known simply as K.L. Saigal, he was a singer and actor in Hindi movies, during the black-and-white era. People believe that he was the first 'superstar' in Hindi cinema. His songs were wildly popular, and people know them even now.

DEEN BANDHU SHARMA

He was an award-winning writer. He won the Sahitya Akademi Award—a prestigious award for literature.

PANDIT SHIVKUMAR SHARMA

He is a great santoor player, who has composed and performed some magical melodies that transport you to the valleys of Kashmir. He has won many awards. His sons also play the santoor.

DINA NATH WALLI

He is one of Kashmir's greatest painters. He recreated his homeland's beauty in his paintings. Having lived in Srinagar for most of his childhood, the valleys and mountains of the region are reflected beautifully in his work.

VIDHU VINOD CHOPRA

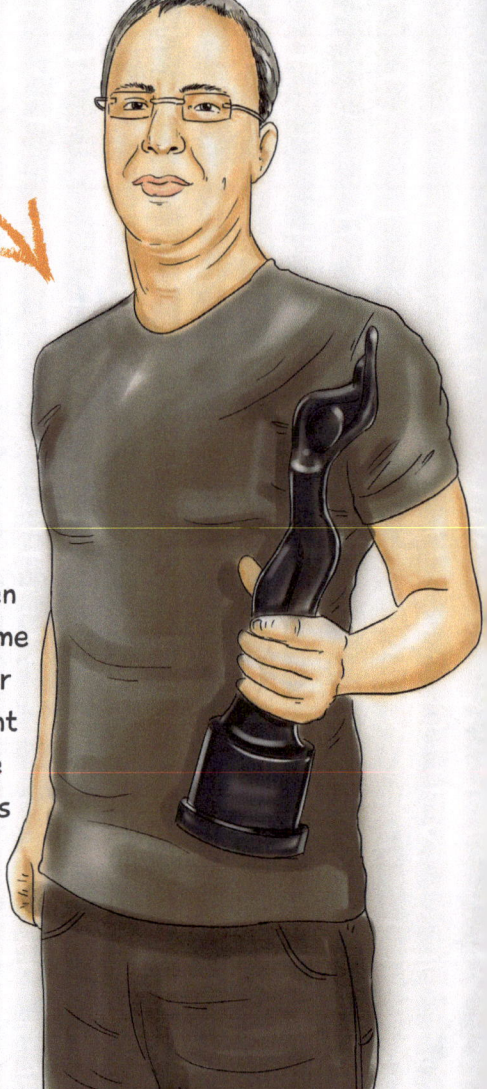

This famous film director has directed and written screenplays for some of the most popular Hindi films of recent times. Some of the blockbusters he has worked on are the Munnabhai series and the path-breaking movie 3 Idiots.

SPOT THE CELEBRITIES

Look! Here are some celebrities from all over India. Draw a circle around the ones from Jammu and Kashmir and write down what they are famous for. If you know any of the other people, write down what they are known for too!

Once upon a time . . .

Oh, look! Here's a lovely place to sit and take in the scenery. Daadu, can you tell us a story from Jammu and Kashmir please?

Of course I can. So just sit back and enjoy this story about a clever astrologer.

THE CLEVER ASTROLOGER

Once upon a time, in the valleys of Kashmir lived a poor man called Manut. He had hardly any money to feed his family. One day he took his wife to the neighbouring village, where the king was hosting a big feast for his daughter's wedding. He hoped to get a job working at the feast.

Luckily, both he and his wife got jobs in the royal kitchen. But everyone ignored Manut because he didn't look very smart.

Manut felt despondent. *People ignore me because they think I am stupid. Well, the time has come for me to teach them a lesson and take matters into my own hands,* he thought.

He devised a plan and told his wife about it. 'From now on, we must pretend that I am an astrologer. I want you to go to the court tomorrow and tell the king the same.'

That night Manut went to the royal stables and led the king's favourite horse to a hiding place in the forest. He left the horse there, tied to a tree.

The next day, when the king found out that his horse had disappeared, he was distraught. He announced a reward of a purseful of gold to whoever found it.

Manut's wife, Chand Bibi, went to the court as her husband had told her to do.

'Your Highness,' she said, 'my husband is an astrologer. He can help you find your horse.'

Manut was summoned. He pretended to do some complicated calculations and finally snapped his fingers.

'Your Highness,' he said, 'your horse is hidden near a stream in the forest.' The king sent his people out at once and, to his joy, the horse was exactly where Manut had said it would be.

'You and your wife shall live in the royal quarters,' the king announced to Manut. Manut and Chand Bibi lived in great luxury for the next several months.

One day, a treasure chest was taken from the royal treasury. A woman called Jivha, which means 'tongue' in the local language, had stolen it, but nobody knew this.

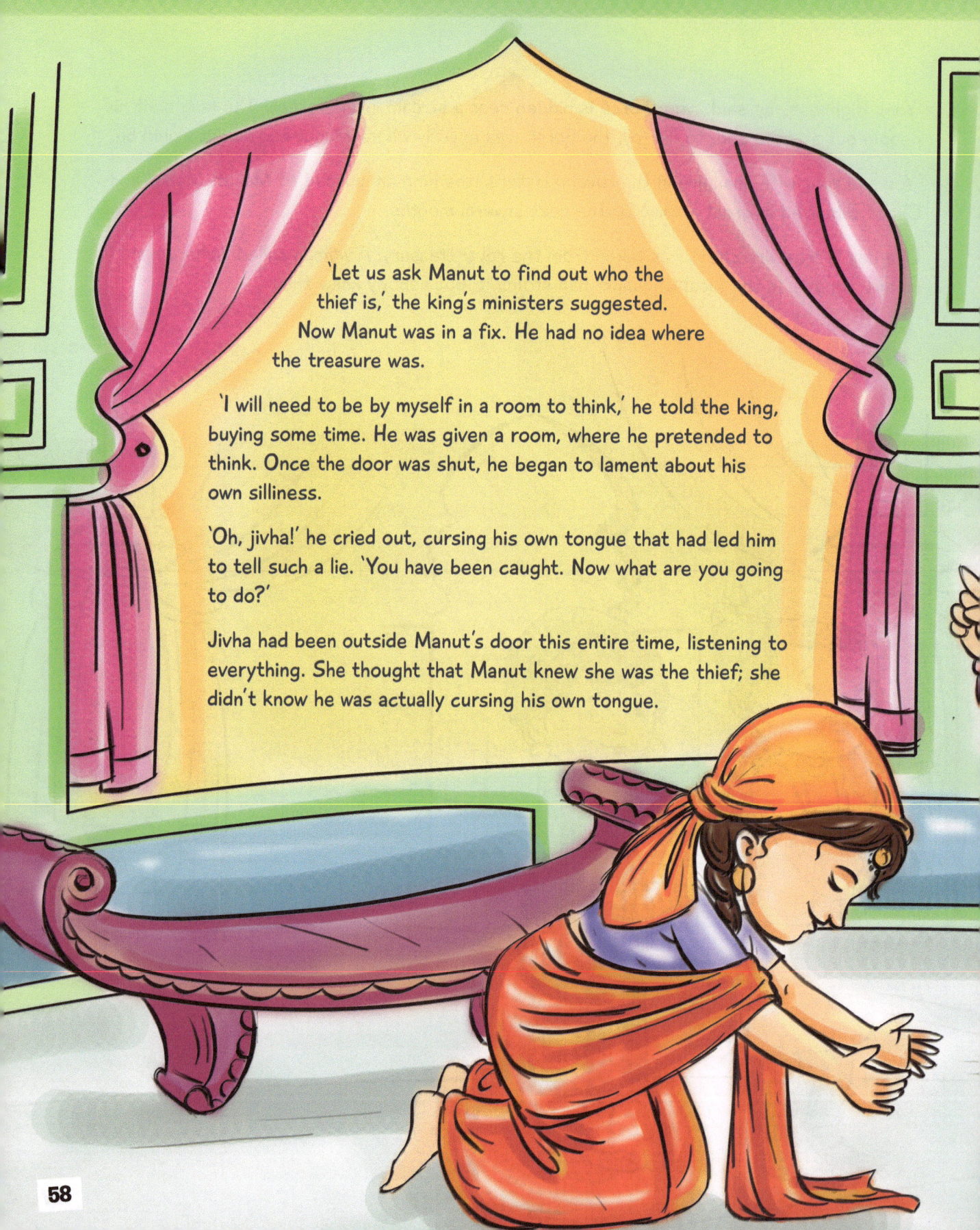

'Let us ask Manut to find out who the thief is,' the king's ministers suggested. Now Manut was in a fix. He had no idea where the treasure was.

'I will need to be by myself in a room to think,' he told the king, buying some time. He was given a room, where he pretended to think. Once the door was shut, he began to lament about his own silliness.

'Oh, jivha!' he cried out, cursing his own tongue that had led him to tell such a lie. 'You have been caught. Now what are you going to do?'

Jivha had been outside Manut's door this entire time, listening to everything. She thought that Manut knew she was the thief; she didn't know he was actually cursing his own tongue.

She rushed into the room and fell at Manut's feet. 'Forgive me, Manut,' she cried. 'Don't tell the king it was me. I will give you anything you want.'

And so Manut was saved once again. But now he had become wise. He told the king he had to visit an ailing relative, took all the gold he had collected and left the kingdom with Chand Bibi, never to be seen again.

And as for Jivha, she thanked her stars for her narrow escape and never forgot Manut for as long as she lived.

TRAVEL DIARY

Have you enjoyed this trip to Jammu and Kashmir with your friends Mishki and Pushka—and, of course, with Daadu Dolma?

Now you can make your own Jammu and Kashmir diary. And if you ever visit Jammu and Kashmir, make sure you take pictures and put them in the photo box.

The first place I would visit in Jammu and Kashmir:

_____

If I were a farmer, I would grow:

_____

The one dish I am definitely going to eat:

_____

The monument I think is the most interesting:

_____

The one famous person from Jammu and Kashmir I would love to meet:

_____

I think the most interesting historical figure from Jammu and Kashmir is:

_____

The festival from Jammu and Kashmir that I think is the most fun:

_____

The five words that I think describe Jammu and Kashmir the best are:

_____

_____

_____

_____

_____

My Jammu and Kashmir memories:

ANSWERS

page 9 HIDDEN RIVERS

T	A	W	I	H	G	F	D	S	A
A	D	C	H	E	N	A	B	O	T
S	F	G	H	J	K	L	P	I	R
A	J	H	E	L	U	M	Y	U	E
S	D	F	I	N	D	U	S	Q	W
F	D	O	D	A	G	H	J	K	L
D	M	N	B	V	D	R	A	S	Z
S	Q	M	A	R	K	H	A	X	C

page 11 WHAT'S ODD

POTATO, COCONUT, TURTLE

page 15 HIDDEN WORDS

Here are some of the words you can form: ban, boa, cab, cam, can, cob, con, ham, jam, lob, loo, man, ran, mob, rob, ram, balm, boom, boon, room, calm, clam, clan, coal, comb, corn, halo, lamb, moan, moon

page 17 RHYME TIME

RULE: COOL, DROOL, FOOL, POOL, SCHOOL, SPOOL
ATTACK: BACK, BLACK, CRACK, HACK, KNACK
QUEEN: BEAN, CLEAN, GLEAN, KEEN, SCENE

page 21 MATCH THEM RIGHT

How are you?— Tohy ch'ivaa vaarai?; Sorry—Maap' keuriv; What's your name?— Twahi kyaa ch'u naav?; Please—Meharbenee; Thank you—Shukriya

page 25 ALL MIXED UP

HAFIZA, ROUF, KUD

page 27 FESTIVAL MATCH

The end of a month of fasting—Eid-ul-Fitr; A three-month festival—Vaishno Devi; The victory of good over evil—Dussehra; A festival also called Ziarat—Urs; A big Buddhist festival—Hemis

page 31 SHIKARA SURPRISE

page 33 LOST IN THE MAZE

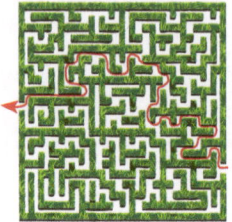

page 35 WHAT COMES NEXT?

A—Blue; B—Red; C—Green

page 39 PRAYING HARD

 A
 B
 C
 D
 E
 F ✓

page 41 CROSSWORD FUN

Across/Down:
1. SAFFRON
2. RICICE (down)
3. F
4. S
5. APPLE
6. JAMES
7. PEACH
8. ORCHARD

page 47 FOOD CODE

LET US EAT

page 53 SPOT THE CELEBRITIES

Vidhu Vinod Chopra, Director-producer; Ustad Allarakha Qureshi, Tabla maestro; Kundan Lal Saigal, Singer-actor; Pandit Shivkumar Sharma, Santoor player; Lalleshwari, Poet-saint